KNOWING GO[

GW00360510

Our Mercitul Judge

Trusting God's Fairness

Six Studies for Groups or Individuals
with Notes for Leaders

Marshall Shelley
Foreword by J. I. Packer

Inter-Varsity Press

INTER-VARSITY PRESS
38 De Montfort Street, Leicester LE1 7GP, England

OUR MERCIFUL JUDGE: *Trusting God's Fairness*
Copyright © 1994 by Marshall Shelley

Unless otherwise stated, Scripture quotations in this publication are from the Holy Bible, New International Version. Copyright © 1973, 1978, 1984 International Bible Society. Published in Great Britain by Hodder and Stoughton Ltd.

First published in the USA by Zondervan Publishing House in 1994

First British edition 1995

British Library Cataloguing in Publication Data

A catalogue record for this book is available from the British Library.

ISBN 0-85111-353-2

Typeset and printed in the United States of America

Inter-Varsity Press is the book-publishing division of the Universities and Colleges Christian Fellowship (formerly the Inter-Varsity Fellowship), a student movement linking Christian Unions in universities and colleges throughout the United Kingdom and the Republic of Ireland and a member movement of the International Fellowship of Evangelical Students. For information about local and national activities write to UCCF, 38 De Montfort Street, Leicester LE1 7GP.

95 96 97 98 99 00 / DP / 6 5 4 3 2 1

Contents

Foreword

One big difference between our current culture and that of a century ago is that the Victorians saw life in terms of roles, while we see it in terms of relationships. Real life, we say, is a matter of relationships, for roles minimize personal involvement while relationships maximize it.

In saying this, we speak more Christian truth than perhaps we realize. For real life according to the Bible means relating not just to other people but also to the personal God who made us. We live and move and exist in him, and it is both scandalous and impoverishing when we ignore him.

Who is he? The startling truth is that he is a *society*. The Father, Son, and Holy Spirit share with each other an intimate and loving relationship. Yet in the unity of their interpersonal life, they constitute a single divine being. God is they, a society and a team, and they are he, the only God there is.

A mystery? An inexplicable reality? Yes, but a life-giving one. It is our privilege not simply to acknowledge the truth of the Trinity but also to enter into a Spirit-sustained relationship with the Father and the Son—a relationship which from one standpoint is *eternal life*, and from another is *knowing God*.

Knowing people involves, first, knowing facts about them and, second, making their acquaintance. How deep our relationship goes depends on how much empathy we have, how many concerns and interests we share, and how much we seek to exalt the one we love. It is the same with knowing God.

The Bible is God's communication to all who hear or read it. Through its varied contents the Triune Lord tells us about himself and calls us to himself. A proper understanding of the Bible will focus at every point on both the information about God and the invitation to know him.

Knowing God Bible Studies are designed to help you achieve this focus. I heartily recommend them. They generate vision, insight, wisdom, and devotion in equal quantities. Use them and you will be blessed.

J. I. Packer

Knowing God Bible Studies

Every Christian desires a deeper, more personal relationship with God. We long to know him better, to feel his presence, and to experience his power in our lives. Jesus himself tells us, "This is eternal life: that they may know you, the only true God, and Jesus Christ, whom you have sent" (John 17:3).

Knowing God Bible Studies can help you build greater intimacy with God. The series explores who God is and how you can know him better. Each guide focuses on a specific attribute of God, such as his love, his faithfulness, or his mercy. The studies are warm and practical and personal—yet they are firmly grounded in Scripture.

The Knowing God series has been field tested in churches across America, representing a wide variety of denominations. This time-intensive process ensures that the guides have solid biblical content, consistent quality, easy-to-use formats, and helpful leader's notes.

Knowing God Bible Studies are designed to be flexible. You can use the guides in any order that is best for you or your group. They are ideal for Sunday-school classes, small groups, one-on-one relationships, or as materials for your quiet times.

Because each guide contains only six studies, you can easily explore more than one attribute of God. In a Sunday-school class, any two guides can be combined for a quarter (twelve weeks), or the entire series can be covered in a year.

Each study deliberately focuses on a limited number of passages, usually only one or two. That allows you to see each passage in its context, avoiding the temptation of prooftexting and the frustration of "Bible hopscotch" (jumping from verse to verse). If you would like to look up additional passages, a Bible concordance will give the most help.

Knowing God Bible Studies help you *discover* what the Bible says rather than simply *telling* you the answers. The questions encourage you to think and to explore options rather than merely to fill in the blanks with one-word answers.

Leader's notes are provided in the back of each guide. They show how to lead a group discussion, provide additional information on questions, and suggest ways to deal with problems that may come up in the discussion. With such helps, someone with little or no experience can lead an effective study.

SUGGESTIONS FOR INDIVIDUAL STUDY

1. Begin each study with prayer. Ask God to help you understand the passage and to apply it to your life.

2. A good modern translation, such as the *New International Version*, the *New American Standard Bible*, or the *New Revised Standard Version*, will give you the most help. Questions in this guide, however, are based on the *New International Version*.

3. Read and reread the passage(s). You must know what the passage says before you can understand what it means and how it applies to you.

4. Write your answers in the space provided in the study guide. This will help you to clearly express your understanding of the passage.

5. Keep a Bible dictionary handy. Use it to look up any unfamiliar words, names, or places.

1. Come to the study prepared. Careful preparation will greatly enrich your time in group discussion.

2. Be willing to join in the discussion. The leader of the group will not be lecturing but will encourage people to discuss what they have learned in the passage. Plan to share what God has taught you in your individual study.

3. Stick to the passage being studied. Base your answers on the verses being discussed rather than on outside authorities such as commentaries or your favorite author or speaker.

4. Try to be sensitive to the other members of the group. Listen attentively when they speak, and be affirming whenever you can. This will encourage more hesitant members of the group to participate.

5. Be careful not to dominate the discussion. By all means participate! But allow others to have equal time.

6. If you are the discussion leader, you will find additional suggestions and helpful ideas in the leader's notes at the back of the guide.

Introducing Our Merciful Judge

This series of studies was born out of an intense personal search to understand the ways of God, to glimpse his eternal purposes in circumstances that, from a human point of view, did not seem fair.

In March 1990, our daughter Mandy was born. Amid the happiness surrounding her successful birth, the doctors told us she had microcephaly (small brain). We'd never heard the term before. Little did we know how Mandy's condition would affect our lives.

In Mandy's case, the microcephaly produced severe and profound retardation. She was never able to crawl, to sit up, to utter any words, to use her hands to grasp. She suffered frequent seizures. We never knew if she could see or hear. The only response we ever saw from her was occasionally when we would give her a bath—a few times she would visibly relax in the warm water. Eventually she was unable to swallow effectively enough to sustain herself, so she had to be fed through a tube surgically implanted into her stomach.

As my wife, Susan, and I cared for her, we wondered about God's purposes. And many of our friends asked us the questions we were asking ourselves: Why would God allow—no, assign—such a severe condition to a child? (There was no known cause for Mandy's microcephaly, except for God's design.) What is her future? Where does the strength come from to care for her?

The only answers that came close to satisfying our confusion centered around God's unexplainable will, his gift of the church to embody his love and care, and the hope of the resurrection.

Then, in November 1991, our son Toby was born. We learned during the pregnancy that he had a chromosomal abnormality called Trisomy 13, a condition the doctors had described as "incompatible with life." He lived two minutes. He spent his entire earthly life on Susan's chest.

Along with the waves of grief, the questions again swept over us: What kind of God creates a child to live two minutes? Genetic tests indicated no relationship between Mandy's condition and Toby's. Both cases were "flukes," design flaws in nature. Where is the fairness in all of this? We reeled under the sadness.

Three months later, in February 1992, we were hit again when Mandy developed a pneumonia that her body didn't have the strength to shake. After eight days in the hospital, she died. Even though, as Christians, we were convinced Mandy was in heaven with Jesus, we missed her deeply. For two years, our lives had revolved around her. Now our house, our arms, our laps, seemed so empty.

This series of studies was written within two years of our children's deaths. It was no academic exercise. It was part of our desperate turning to Scripture to discover whether God is trustworthy, whether the Judge of the Universe can be counted on to treat people right.

These six studies focus on six sections of the Bible that offered us fresh glimpses of how God works.

I hope you will find, as we did, that even if some of our experiences are severe, God is worthy of our trust.

Marshall Shelley

1

The Most Deadly Temptation
Genesis 3

Who's worse: a clerk at the deli who slyly rests her thumb on the scale as she weighs your purchase, or a deli manager who adjusts the scale so it reads heavier than the product actually weighs?

Granted, both are deceitful. But with the clerk, at least there's still a trustworthy standard of measurement. Remove the thumb, and you can get an accurate reading. The manager has destroyed not only his own integrity, but the integrity of the scale. The measure of truth has itself become unreliable.

The only way integrity can be restored is for the scale to be recalibrated to accuracy.

Why is the question of God's fairness so crucial? Because if God is not fair and trustworthy, the scales of eternity are unreliable. With what can they be recalibrated?

It's no coincidence that the first temptation mentioned in the Bible is the most deadly—an attempt to cast doubt on God's goodness and trustworthiness.

1. What's one law that you're glad is on the books?

Innocent until proven guilty.

2. Read Genesis 3. As the first woman, living in a perfect environment, how was Eve different from us?

How do these differences make the temptation she faced less cluttered and easier to understand?

3. Temptation first approaches Eve in the form of a serpent. What tactic lies behind the serpent's seemingly innocent question (v. 1)?

4. How does the tempter misquote God's instruction (see Gen. 2:16)?

5. Why do you suppose the tempter focuses Eve's attention on the one tree, and not the whole orchard she could eat from?

6. Eve does not accurately report God's command (v. 3). Why do you suppose she adds the part about "not even touching it"?

7. The tempter says that disobeying God's instruction will not have any bad consequences (v. 4). In what ways are people today led to believe that sin has no consequences?

8. How does the tempter try to question God's motives (v. 5)?

9. Why is planting doubts about a person's motives one of the most insidious, dangerous actions?

10. If you doubt God's goodness, what deadly effect does that have on you?

11. What's the real sin here—a piece of fruit? Or something else?

12. Why is trust just as important to God as obedience?

13. Do you view God as someone you can trust—even when he seems to withhold something good from you? Explain.

Do you see his commands for you as love or unreasonable limits? Why?

Memory Verse

"And the LORD God said, 'The man has now become like one of us, knowing good and evil. He must not be allowed to reach out his hand and take also from the tree of life and eat, and live forever.'"

Genesis 3:22

BETWEEN STUDIES

Investigate the full effects of this first act of rebellion and distrust against God. Read Romans 5:12–21 and 1 Corinthians 15:20–26, 45–49. How has God acted to reverse the effects of that sin and mistrust?

2

When Life Seems Unfair
Job 1-2

"Early to bed, early to rise, makes a man healthy, wealthy, and wise." Do you believe that? Or is that old proverb a myth?

One wag paraphrased it this way: "Early to rise, early to bed, makes a man nothing but socially dead."

What if someone has all the right habits but still loses health, wealth, and wisdom? Having the right sleeping pattern may not be sufficient to restore what has been lost.

In the book of Job, we read the story of a man who loses his possessions, his children, and his health. While the book doesn't report if Job's wisdom was lost, too, we do know that he had many unanswered questions as the seeming unfairness of his condition overwhelmed him.

The story of Job is a timeless case study in the mystery of suffering and the mysterious purposes of God.

1. What would you say are the key factors contributing to success?

   Which of these factors are outside a person's control, and which are solely up to the individual?

2. Read Job chapters 1 and 2. What was Satan's basic point (1:9–11)?

3. Do you think it's generally true that people believe in God only for protection and prosperity? Explain.

4. Does prosperity tend to keep people trusting God, or does it tend to distract them from God? Why?

5. Why do you think God allowed Satan to attack Job?

❑ To punish Job?
❑ To strengthen Job?
❑ He couldn't prevent it?
❑ To find out if Job's faith was real?
❑ I don't know.

Explain your answer.

6. What do you find threatens your faith the most?

❑ Financial pressure
❑ Financial prosperity
❑ Life-threatening illness
❑ Continued good health
❑ Natural disaster
❑ The dull routines of daily life
❑ Death
❑ Busyness
❑ Strained or broken relationships

Why is this the greatest threat to your faith?

7. Notice how God restricts Satan's ability to torment Job (1:12; 2:6). What does that say to you about the limits of the trials and difficulties we face?

8. According to 1:22 and 2:10, what determines whether or not Job passes the test?

9. Read the following portions of the book of Job to sample the advice the comforters provided and their conversations with Job:

❑ Job (3:2–10, 23–26)
❑ Eliphaz (4:2–8, 5:3, 8)
❑ Job (6:24–30, 7:12–19)
❑ Bildad (8:2–7, 20)
❑ Job (9:2, 20, 22, 27–35)
❑ Zophar (11:2–6)
❑ Job (16:2–5, 17:1–4)

What was the basic assumption of Job's comforters?

How would you respond to them?

10. What did Job's comforters do right?

11. Job claims he is righteous. His friends claim he's a sinner. Why do you think God later condemns the comforters for what they said (42:7)?

12. How would you describe Job's response to his life situation?

In what ways is he a good model for you when life seems unfair?

Memory Verse

Naked I came from my mother's womb, and naked I will depart. The LORD gave and the LORD has taken away; may the name of the LORD be praised.

Job 1:21

■ BETWEEN STUDIES ■

Sometimes it's hard to trust God when life seems unjust. It wasn't any easier for the individuals in the Bible who lived faithful lives and still didn't reap any benefit for their effort. Read the "Faith Hall of Fame" in Hebrews 11. Why do you think these people continued to trust God even when it cost them their comfort, their security, even their lives?

3

The Source
of Fairness

Job 38-42

The town hall in Copenhagen, Denmark, contains the world's most complicated clock. Constructing it took forty years. The clock has ten faces and fifteen thousand parts. It computes the time of day, the days of the week, the months and years, and movements of the planets for twenty-five hundred years. Some parts of that clock will not move until twenty-five centuries have passed.

The makers proudly say the clock is accurate to two-fifths of a second every three hundred years.

But what's intriguing is that the clock is not perfectly accurate. It loses those two-fifths of a second every three hundred years. The question is: How would anyone know? Who would notice?

The answer: Like all clocks, the timepiece in Copenhagen is regulated by a more precise clock, the universe itself.

The "clock" that God created has billions of moving parts, from subatomic particles to supernova, and it rolls on century after century with movements so reliable that the best efforts of the brightest minds on earth are measured by it.

Just as our understanding of time must be measured against God's standard, so too our understanding fairness must be measured against the source of fairness, God himself.

This study looks at what happens when one man, questioning God, was confronted directly by his Creator.

1. True or false: "Life is fair." Explain your answer.

True or false: "God is fair." Explain your answer.

2. After reflecting on your previous study of the first part of the book of Job, what do you think tormented Job the most about his losses? Why?

3. Read Job chapters 38 and 40.[1] How does God finally respond to Job?

Why do you think he doesn't answer Job's questions directly and point by point?

4. What are some of the elements of nature that overwhelm you?

What do these elements of nature communicate to you about God?

5. Read Job chapter 42. What has Job learned about himself and about God (vv. 1–6)?

How can Job's experience help us when we feel that God has treated us unfairly?

6. After God is done speaking to Job, what means does God use to restore Job's wealth?

7. Why do you suppose God chooses to work through people?

8. What do you make of the fact that God restores double the livestock, but only the same number of children to Job?

9. Would God still have been Job's friend had he not restored his wealth and family? Explain.

Does God always provide happy endings?

10. After hearing God's words of accusation against Job's comforters, what approach will you take in comforting people you know who are suffering?

Memory Verse

Would you discredit my justice? Would you condemn me to justify yourself?

Job 40:8

BETWEEN STUDIES

Job's "friends" initially took the right approach. They spent time with him, but they did not say a word for seven days and seven nights! (See Job 3:11–13.)

Think of someone you know who is suffering. How can you comfort and support that person this week without offering pious platitudes or simple solutions to their problems?

Note

1. If you have time, read chapters 38–42. For those studying in groups, it would probably be best to read the selected chapters suggested in this study.

4

God's Criteria of Judgment
Romans 2

In the midst of a Little League baseball game, a young batter watched a third pitch cross home plate. "Strike three!" shouted the umpire. "You're out."

The batter stormed back to the bench. "That's not fair," he pouted. "I didn't like any of those pitches."

The coach corrected him. "Whether you liked them or not, they were strikes. You got fairness. If he'd given you more than three strikes to look at, THAT's what wouldn't be fair."

How often we hear someone say, "That's not fair," when the person really means, "I didn't get my way."

This notion of fairness is one of the first concepts children seem to grasp. It continues through adulthood, too, although the language may vary. Among adults, we hear things like, "I deserve one," or "I owe it to myself," or "I demand my rights."

What was the young batter's assumption about fairness? He assumed things were fair only if they went his way. Fairness doesn't mean every outcome turns out the way we want. But it does mean that the rules are clear.

This study is a look at what God considers life's "strike zone."

1. What are the perks of belonging to a church or some other form of Christian community?

Do you see any spiritual dangers of belonging to such a group?

2. Read Romans 2:1–16. What type of person is Paul addressing in this passage?

How would you describe the person's attitude?

3. How can Paul be so sure that those who judge others are guilty of the same sins (vv. 1–3)?

4. Why might a religious person feel free to condemn others while practicing the same sins he condemns (vv. 3–4)?

How does this kind of attitude "show contempt for the riches of God's kindness, tolerance, and patience" (v. 4)?

5. In what ways do we Christians sometimes condemn in others what we quietly permit among ourselves?

6. According to Paul, what is the basis on which God is going to reward or punish someone (vv. 6–10)?

7. What do you think is involved in "persistence in doing good" and in seeking "glory, honor, and immortality" (v. 7)?

8. In this context, what does Paul mean when he says, "God does not show favoritism" (v. 11)? Does that mean everyone is given the same advantages in life?

9. How will those who know God's law be judged by a different standard than those who are ignorant of Scripture (vv. 12–15)?

Does the fact that there are two standards seem fair to you? Explain.

10. This chapter describes the criteria by which God will judge the world (v. 16). But if we look ahead to the conclusion of Paul's argument, what will the verdict be for *anyone* who is judged by God's high standards (3:19–20)?

11. People often think they want nothing but justice from God. How does Paul help us realize that what we really need is God's mercy and grace?

12. Thank God for the fact that he can remain just and yet still justify those who have broken his law (see Rom. 3:26). Ask him for strength to obey his law even though it is not the basis of your salvation.

Memory Verse

You, therefore, have no excuse, you who pass judgment on someone else, for at whatever point you judge the other, you are condemning yourself, because you who pass judgment do the same things.

Romans 2:1

BETWEEN STUDIES

Investigate further what God considers important. Read Amos 5 and list the items at the top of God's agenda for his people. Then list what ways you can begin living out those purposes.

5

Undeserved Love

Romans 5-8

Comedian Jack Benny was once given an award. "I don't deserve this," he deadpanned. "But then I have arthritis, and I don't deserve that either."

His point, humorously made, is that both bad things and good things happen to us. If we're going to question the unfairness of life and the difficulties God allows into our lives, we must also consider the undeserved gifts that God sends our way.

The most important of these undeserved gifts is something the Bible calls "grace." It's God's free gift of salvation given to people who have not earned it.

This study investigates the happy unfairness of God's generosity to us.

1. When have you, like Jack Benny, been given something from others that you don't deserve?

2. Read Romans 5:1–11.[1] Paul describes salvation as "reconciliation" or making peace with God (v. 1). How does this peace happen?

3. The phrase translated "gained access" in verse 2 is a Greek word that refers to a harbor or haven that provides ships a safe place to reach port. How does that word picture help illustrate what God has done for us?

4. Why do you suppose immediately after verses talking about standing secure and rejoicing "in the hope of the glory of God," the next verses talk about suffering?

How are God's love, suffering, and hope interrelated?

5. What's surprising about the "who" and the "when" in verses 6–8?

6. Now that we have been reconciled to God, how can we be absolutely certain that we will never experience his wrath (vv. 9–11)?

7. Read Romans 6:15–23. After reading this passage, how would you respond to the person who once said, "I love to sin, and God loves to forgive. It's a wonderful relationship."

8. According to Paul we were slaves before we became Christians, and we are still slaves! Yet what are the differences between the two types of slavery and their results?

9. Is holiness (or "sanctification") something that happens to us immediately or eventually (v. 22)? Explain.

10. Read Romans 8:18–25. What frustrates you most about living in a fallen world where sin and evil and decay still have their effect?

11. What does salvation mean in this passage?

12. After considering all three of these Bible passages, is salvation (1) a one-time event in a person's life, (2) an ongoing process, or (3) an eventual goal? Explain.

13. Once you understand the lengths to which God went to provide salvation, how does that affect your attitude toward the "unfairness" of life?

Memory Verse

Very rarely will anyone die for a righteous man, though for a good man someone might possibly dare to die. But God demonstrates his own love for us in this: While we were still sinners, Christ died for us.

Romans 5:7–8

BETWEEN STUDIES

The French painter Georges Seurat used a style known as "pointillism." He painted with dots of color that looked meaningless up close but from a distance blended into a beautiful work of art.

Reflect this week on the fact that many of the seemingly unfair events in our lives—especially those that make us question God's love—may only make sense when we see the "big picture" of God's salvation. Ask God for the grace to trust him when all you see is meaningless "dots."

Note

1. If you have time, read Romans 5–8 in its entirety to see the overall context of Paul's argument. If you are studying in a group, however, it would be best to read only the selected passages in this study.

6

Beyond Fairness

Philippians 2

Some people find that the Bible offends their sense of fairness. The parable of the vineyard workers (Matt. 20), for instance, violates the principle of payment according to work accomplished. Why should everyone get equal pay for unequal work?

A few years ago, a man named Robert De Moor wrote about his family: "Back in Ontario when the apples ripened, Mom would sit all seven of us down, Dad included, with pans and paring knives until the mountain of fruit was reduced to neat rows of filled canning jars. She never bothered keeping track of how many we did, though the younger ones undoubtedly proved more of a nuisance than a help: cut fingers, squabbles over who got which pan, apple core fights.

"But when the job was done, the reward for everyone was the same: the largest chocolate-dipped cone money could buy.

"A stickler might argue it wasn't quite fair since the older ones actually peeled apples. But I can't remember anyone complaining about it."

Just as a family operates under a different set of norms than a corporation, so, too, God's kingdom operates by its own unique standards.

Justice, fairness, and individual rights are important. But to God, there's something even more important than insisting on your rights. Christ himself went beyond fairness to show us an even better way.

---

1. What is your least favorite household chore?

2. Read Philippians 2:1–11. What attitude does the writer, the apostle Paul, want to instill?

3. Someone once said, "You can tell if you're becoming a servant by the way you react when people treat you like one." How did you react most recently while performing your least favorite chore?

4. What's the difference between humility and being a doormat?

5. Verses 6–11 are probably the words to a song the early Christians sang about Jesus. According to this song, who is Jesus?

6. What did Jesus do with his "rights" and his "true identity"?

7. Most gods do not serve. They demand to be served. Why do you suppose Jesus, who is "in very nature God," would come to serve (vv. 6–8)?

8. Can even God force someone to love him? Why or why not?

9. What means did Christ use to communicate the depth of his love for us?

What aspects of his life demonstrate how far he was willing to go?

10. In verses 9–11, what are the results of Christ's obedience?

11. Jesus himself told us, "Whoever exalts himself will be humbled, and whoever humbles himself will be exalted" (Matt. 23:12). How does this warning and promise motivate you to be a servant?

12. Who are some people you've known whom you would describe as true servants?

13. In what specific ways can you, too, be this kind of servant?

Memory Verse

Your attitude should be the same as that of Christ Jesus: Who, being in very nature God, did not consider equality with God something to be grasped, but made himself nothing, taking the very nature of a servant.

Philippians 2:5–7

■ BETWEEN STUDIES ■

Often when we are asked to take the role of a servant, to do some menial or distasteful task, we feel like saying, "That's not fair!" Yet how fair is any sacrifice? In Christ, we see God himself going beyond fairness to love.

This week pick one or two jobs that no one else wants to do (washing the dishes, refilling the coffeemaker, cleaning the toilets, and so on). Ask God for the strength and love to serve others by doing these jobs, realizing that although they are unfulfilling now, God will ultimately reward you for your humble service.

Leader's Notes

L eading a Bible discussion—especially for the first time—can
make you feel both nervous and excited. If you are nervous,
realize that you are in good company. Many biblical leaders,
such as Moses, Joshua, and the apostle Paul, felt nervous and
inadequate to lead others (see, for example, 1 Cor. 2:3). Yet
God's grace was sufficient for them, just as it will be for you.

Some excitement is also natural. Your leadership is a gift to the
others in the group. Keep in mind, however, that other group
members also share responsibility for the group. Your role is
simply to stimulate discussion by asking questions and
encouraging people to respond. The suggestions listed below
can help you to be an effective leader.

**PREPARING
TO LEAD**

1. Ask God to help you understand
and apply the passage to your own
life. Unless that happens, you will
not be prepared to lead others.

2. Carefully work through each question in the study guide.
Meditate and reflect on the passage as you formulate your
answers.

3. Familiarize yourself with the leader's notes for the study.
These will help you understand the purpose of the study

and will provide valuable information about the questions in the study.

4. Pray for the various members of the group. Ask God to use these studies to make you better disciples of Jesus Christ.

5. Before the first meeting, make sure each person has a study guide. Encourage them to prepare beforehand for each study.

LEADING THE STUDY

1. Begin the study on time. If people realize that the study begins on schedule, they will work harder to arrive on time.

2. At the beginning of your first time together, explain that these studies are designed to be discussions, not lectures. Encourage everyone to participate, but realize that some may be hesitant to speak during the first few sessions.

3. Read the introductory paragraph at the beginning of the discussion. This will orient the group to the passage being studied.

4. Read the passage aloud. You may choose to do this yourself, or you might ask for volunteers.

5. The questions in the guide are designed to be used just as they are written. If you wish, you may simply read each one aloud to the group. Or you may prefer to express them in your own words. Unnecessary rewording of the questions, however, is not recommended.

6. Don't be afraid of silence. People in the group may need time to think before responding.

7. Avoid answering your own questions. If necessary, rephrase a question until it is clearly understood. Even an eager group will quickly become passive and silent if they think the leader will do most of the talking.

8. Encourage more than one answer to each question. Ask, "What do the rest of you think?" or "Anyone else?" until several people have had a chance to respond.

9. Try to be affirming whenever possible. Let people know you appreciate their insights into the passage.

10. Never reject an answer. If it is clearly wrong, ask, "Which verse led you to that conclusion?" Or let the group handle the problem by asking them what they think about the question.

11. Avoid going off on tangents. If people wander off course, gently bring them back to the passage being considered.

12. Conclude your time together with conversational prayer. Ask God to help you apply those things that you learned in the study.

13. End on time. This will be easier if you control the pace of the discussion by not spending too much time on some questions or too little on others.

Many more suggestions and helps are found in the book *Leading Bible Discussions* (InterVarsity Press). Reading it would be well worth your time.

The Most Deadly Temptation
GENESIS 3

Purpose: To discover why any attempt to cast doubt on God's goodness and trustworthiness is the most deadly form of temptation.

Question 1 Every study begins with a "warm-up question," which is discussed *before* reading the passage. A warm-up question is designed to do three things.

First, it helps to break the ice. Because a warm-up question doesn't require any knowledge of the passage or any special preparation, it can get people talking and can help them to feel more comfortable with each other.

Second, a warm-up question can motivate people to study the passage at hand. At the beginning of the study, people in the group aren't necessarily ready to jump into the world of the Bible. Their minds may be on other things (their kids, a problem at work, an upcoming meeting) that have nothing to do with the study. A warm-up question can capture their interest and draw them into the discussion by raising important issues related to the study. The question becomes a bridge between their personal lives and the answers found in Scripture.

Third, a good warm-up question can reveal where people's thoughts or feelings need to be transformed by Scripture. That is why it is important to ask the warm-up question *before* reading the passage. The passage might inhibit the spontaneous, honest answers people might have given, because they feel compelled to give biblical answers. The warm-up question allows them to compare their personal thoughts and feelings with what they later discover in Scripture.

Question 2 Eve had no taint of environmental or genetic flaws. She was without sin, without bad influences from her childhood, and without pain in her present circumstances. These factors make this interaction with the serpent a fascinating case study in temptation—what tempts a person without emotional baggage? In this case, we get to the essence of temptation.

Question 3 The Tempter comes in disguise—as a serpent. Not overtly. In this case as a comfortable companion. Mephistopheles says, in *Faust,* "The people do not even know the Devil is there, even when he has them by the throat."

His tactic is to ask seemingly innocent questions about God. He's a religious devil. He doesn't say, "Give me a half hour of your time, and I will damn you for eternity." No, he begins by questioning God's instructions and sowing seeds of doubt about God's generosity.

Question 5 What once was out of bounds becomes the thing you desire most of all. That preoccupation may become the thing that destroys you.

Question 7 One of today's most common temptations is to take sin lightly. The cosmetics industry uses words like "Seduction" or "My Sin" as names for cologne. The entertainment media often portray people who violate God's commands without any apparent ill effect. In a similar way, the serpent in Genesis communicates the idea that judgment will never come.

Question 8 He suggests that God doesn't really have Adam and Eve's best interests in mind. He tries to drive a wedge between them and God, making them suspicious of God's direction in their lives.

Question 9 If you successfully get someone to question another person's motives, no matter what the person does, it's not good enough. Even if they do something good, you'll suspect that they're doing it just to fool you for their own selfish, possibly evil, purposes. When you destroy trust, you've poisoned the well that waters the relationship.

Question 11 The fruit is a peripheral issue. The core sin is our central attitude toward God. The real sin is denying God's goodness, doubting that his purposes are for our own good. Such sin prevents us from trusting God.

STUDY TWO

When Life Seems Unfair
JOB 1–2

Purpose: To explore the mystery of suffering and how it relates to the mysterious purposes of God.

Questions 2–3 Many people are fair-weather believers. Adversity tests faith, revealing whether our belief in God is made of tougher stuff than simply a wishful means of prosperity and protection.

Question 4 Satan claims prosperity kept Job faithful to God. But prosperity can just as easily cause people to neglect God, to feel as if they are self-sufficient.

Question 5 There are at least two other possibilities:

❑ To demonstrate whether Job loved his possessions more than God.

❑ To see if Job would continue to trust God when he had no compelling reason to do so. This is the real test of faithfulness—whether a person will remain true when the pressure is on to betray or deny his loyalty to another.

Question 7 God establishes the boundaries, and he does not allow Satan to attack us beyond what we are able to bear. The suffering we endure may be terrible, but just as God refused to allow Satan to go beyond a certain point, so he continues to refuse to allow Satan to attack us beyond what we can withstand.

Question 8 Though Job had lost family, possessions, and his health, he retained his belief that God is just. As we saw in Study 1, Satan's design is to get people to believe that God is not good. Job continues to acknowledge God's authority and power. Job passes the test, choosing to worship God for who he is and not for what he gives.

Question 9 You might assign these passages to various members of your group, asking them to read in turn.

Job's comforters assumed that life is fair, that all consequences are a result of human behavior. They didn't take into account God's mysterious purposes.

Question 10 At least they came! In the end (42:7), God condemns what they said, but he doesn't condemn what they did. They at least reached out to Job.

Question 11 Job admitted that he was sinner. When he claimed to be righteous, he meant that he could not see his sin as the reason for the disaster that came upon him. And with that, God agrees. His comforters had self-righteously criticized him for behavior no worse than their own.

Question 12 Job did not hide his grief or deny his pain. He displayed a healthy questioning of the circumstances, but alongside his clear expression of suffering, he refused to give up or to stop trusting God's continuing work in his life.

STUDY THREE

The Source of Fairness

JOB 38–42

Purpose: To realize that our understanding of fairness must be measured against the source of fairness, God himself.

Question 3 Ultimately, the only answer is that God is in charge, that he's the only one who sees the "big picture" (encompassing the entire universe, past, present, and future), and that he does whatever he knows is best. Humans cannot always understand God's actions. They can only trust that his purposes are good.

Question 7 Consider the importance God apparently attaches to our compassion and generosity toward one another. When we help those who are hurting, we become God's hands and arms. We are privileged to become the instruments God uses to accomplish his purpose.

Question 8 If God intended to double Job's previous possessions, he had to provide twice the number of cattle, but since the children who died were living in eternity (and Job would see them again), Job got twice the children by having only seven more.

STUDY FOUR

God's Criteria of Judgment
ROMANS 2

Purpose: To consider the standards and requirements by which God will judge the world through Jesus Christ.

Question 1 Although there are many benefits of belonging to a Christian community, it's possible to rely on the group for your relationship with God rather than truly seeking a personal relationship with him.

Question 2 Paul addresses Jews (see v. 17), who felt their special "chosen people" status with God made them morally superior to those sinners Paul describes in the first chapter of Romans.

Question 3 A self-righteous attitude is just as distasteful to God as the attitude of contempt toward holiness from those who have rejected God's ways. In addition, those who judge others may be living by a double standard—condemning behavior in others that they rationalize for themselves (see 2:17–24). In Romans 3:19–20 Paul asserts that on the Judgment Day "every mouth will be silenced and the whole world [including the self-righteous] held accountable to God" for their sin.

Question 6 On whether the person's life is focused on God's agenda—"glory, honor, and immortality"—or whether the person's life is marked by self-seeking, rejection of the truth, and following evil (vv. 7–8).

Question 8 Some people are raised in godly homes, surrounded by love, and learn about God early and naturally; others are raised in homes where God's name is used only in anger. Obviously some people have better opportunities to learn about God. Paul's point is that God does not reward people for their family of origin (Jew or Gentile), but only how a person responds to God's agenda.

Question 9 Those who know God's law will be judged by the standards of that written revelation. But even those who do not know the written law of God have an unwritten law within their hearts. We might call it an instinctive sense of right and wrong. In addition, all people can see the evidence of the Creator. And all people know about death. God expects people, even if they've never read the Bible, to pursue right and to aim for "glory, honor, and immortality."

Question 11 Those who demand God's justice will get it on the Judgment Day, but that justice will also condemn them because of their sin. Throughout Romans 1–4 Paul's point is that no one measures up to God's high standards, and therefore no one will be saved by "law." Instead, we must admit our guilt and receive the grace and mercy God offers us in Jesus Christ (see Rom. 3:21–31).

Yet the fact that we will not be saved by keeping the law does not mean that we are free to disregard God's standards and live a lifestyle characterized by sin. According to Paul and the other New Testament writers, there is no such thing as faith that does not reveal itself in good works. And there are no truly good works that do not emerge out of faith. Faith and works are interwoven. Without outward evidence that our life is directed Godward, chances are slim that there's any real faith on the inside (see James 2:14–26).

Undeserved Love
ROMANS 5

Purpose: To investigate the happy unfairness of God's generosity to us.

Question 3 God has built the structure that rescues us from the destructive waves. He, not we in our little ship, has provided the salvation we need. Through Christ, we have a safe access to God.

Question 4 The word "suffering" can also be translated "pressure" or "stress." The word "perseverance" means joyful endurance or determination to overcome the situation. "Character" refers to what results from testing—silver, for instance, that has been tested and purged of impurities is called "sterling." When pressure is met with godly perseverance, the result is sterling character. "Hope" is what allows a person to see a crisis not as a sure defeat but as a wonderful opportunity. Someone once observed, "I do not like crises, but I do like the opportunities they provide." That statement can only come from someone who has hope.

Question 5 God is the one who rescues us, and he does it not because we're good people but despite the fact that we're sinful, rebellious, self-centered people.

Question 8 There are many differences between the two types of slavery and their results. One slavery is to sin, and the other is to righteousness. One is characterized by impurity and ever-increasing wickedness, and the other is characterized by righteousness and holiness. One is a wage that we earn, while the other is a gift that is undeserved. And one leads to death, while the other leads to eternal life.

According to Paul, our slavery to sin and its terrible consequences ended forever when we trusted in Christ (vv. 17–18). From that moment on, we became "slaves to righteousness." When we sin as Christians, we do not suddenly revert back to being slaves of sin—that life is gone forever. Rather, we make the mistake of obeying something that is no longer our master and that has no authority or ultimate power over us.

Question 12 Trick question! It's all three. Salvation means:

- ❏ "I have been saved from sin's penalty." That's called justification.
- ❏ "I am being saved from sin's power." That's called sanctification.
- ❏ "One day, in eternity, I will be saved from sin's presence." That's called glorification.

Salvation, that wonderful relationship with God, involves all three of these aspects.

Beyond Fairness

PHILIPPIANS 2

Purpose: To discover how Christ went beyond fairness to show us a better way.

Question 4 A doormat lets others do whatever they want—even if it's destructive. The humble person gently but firmly obeys God. True humility is having an accurate perspective about ourselves and our position before God. We are sinners, unable to save ourselves, totally at the mercy of God. But because Christ saved us, at the cost of his own life, we recognize how valuable we are to him. Since we owe him our lives, in gratitude we're to live as he did—selflessly, giving ourselves for the good of others.

Question 6 Christ, who was equal with God, gave up his rights and the full exercise of his powers as God. He voluntarily limited himself to become human so he could save the human race from the contamination of sin. As Paul describes it elsewhere, "Though he was rich, yet for your sakes he became poor, so that you through his poverty might become rich" (2 Cor. 8:9).

Question 7 God's favor can't be "grasped" (v. 6). Remember those in the Bible who tried to become like God or snatch his authority: Adam and Eve, the builders of the Tower of Babel, Lucifer? They failed. In a strange twist, God says that only those don't try to achieve glory for themselves will receive lasting honor and glory.

Question 8 Love can't be taken by force. Words like "rape" and "seduction" describe the forcible and manipulative attempts to gain someone else's love. But true love can't be extracted from someone else—it can only be given, freely, by one person to another. Through Christ, God freely demonstrates his love for us. We can choose to accept and return that love, or we can reject God's love. God will not force himself upon anyone.

As Reinhold Niebuhr once said, "You may be able to compel people to maintain certain minimum standards by stressing duty, but the highest moral and spiritual achievements depend not upon a push but a pull. People must be charmed into righteousness."

God "charms" us by showing us the extent of his love for us.

Question 9 His birth in a manger, his life among the poor and despised, his death as a criminal—all testify to the depth of his love.

Question 10 Because of Christ's obedience and servanthood, God honors him with a name that is above all other names. His name, Jesus, means "salvation." The name Lord means "ruler" or "boss" over all.

C. S. Lewis describes this elevation of Christ in his book, *Miracles:* "In the Christian story God descends to reascend. . . . He goes down to come up again and bring the whole ruined world up with Him. One has the picture of a strong man stooping lower and lower to get himself underneath some great complicated burden. He must stoop in order to lift, he must almost disappear under the load before he incredibly straightens his back and marches off with the whole mass swaying on his shoulders." Lewis goes on to say:

> Or one may think of a diver, first reducing himself to nakedness, then glancing in mid-air, then gone with a splash, vanished, rushing down through green and warm water into black and cold water, down through increasing pressure into the death-like region of ooze and slime and old decay; then up again, back to color and light, his lungs almost bursting, till suddenly he breaks the surface again, holding in this hand the dripping, precious thing that he went down to recover. He and it are both colored now that they have come up into the light: down below, where it lay colorless in the dark, he lost his color, too."

(C. S. Lewis, *Miracles* [London: Collins/Fontana Books, 1960], pp. 115–16).

NOTES

NOTES

NOTES

NOTES